The Story of THE

Resurrection Eggs®

in **Rhyme** and **Song**

Miss Patty Cake™

Opens up the Wonder of the Easter Story

JEAN THOMASON AND NANCY GORDON

INTEGRITY®
PUBLISHERS
Nashville

The Story of the Resurrection Eggs in Rhyme and Song

Copyright © 2003 Jean Thomason and Nancy Gordon.
Published by Integrity Publishers, a division of Integrity Media, Inc. 5250 Virginia Way, Suite.110, Brentwood, TN 37027.

Resurrection Eggs © 1994, 2003, FamilyLife. Used by permission of FamilyLife™. All rights reserved.

"PattyCake Praise" by Nancy Gordon and Chris Springer, © 1994 Integrity's Hosanna!
Music ACAP & Integrity's Praise! Music/BMI, c/o Integrity Media, Inc. 1000 Cody Road, Mobile, AL 36695

"Shout Hosanna" by Nancy Gordon and Steve Merkel, © 2002 Mother's Heart Music
(administered by Integrity's Hosanna! Music)/ASCAP & Integrity's Hosanna!
Music/ASCAP, c/o Integrity Media, Inc. 1000 Cody Road, Mobile, AL 36695

"Jesus Said Yes" by Nancy Gordon, Steve Merkel and Jean Thomason, © 2002 Mother's Heart Music (administered by Integrity's Hosanna! Music)/ASCAP & Integrity's Hosanna! Music/ASCAP, c/o Integrity Media, Inc. 1000 Cody Road, Mobile, AL 36695

"Mighty Resurrection Day" by Nancy Gordon, © 1998 by Pilot Pint Music (ASCAP). All rights reserved.
Administered by the Copyright Company, 1025 16th Ave., South, Nashville, TN 37212.

"Colors Numbers/ABC's" by Steve Merkel and Jean Thomason, © 2002 Integrity's Hosanna! Music/ASCAP,
c/o Integrity Media, Inc. 1000 Cody Road, Mobile, AL 36695

Cover and Interior design: Russ McIntosh, The Office of Bill Chiaravalle, www.officeofbc.com
Photography: Ric Moore

ACKNOWELEDGMENTS
This book is dedicated to Mom Bebe, who imparted to me the essence of Miss PattyCake, and to Chris, Marilyn, and Christopher for sharing me with so many children...I love you. And to my fabulous family and to my friends: Robin, Mary, Jennifer, and Michael, for BELIEVING; and to Karl, Steve, and Matt for vision, direction, encouragement, and endurance. Thank you all.
-Jean Thomason

Thanks Bob, Nolan, Gerritt, Hannah, Stuart, April, and Mama for being my great family. This book is dedicated to all of you. I would also like to say thank-you to Integrity Music for believing in the value of this ministry to children. For my mentors and friends...John, Claire, Steve, Chris, Gerrit, Himmie, Hamp, Barbara, F.G., Susan, John, Sue, and Julie. Thanks for all your love, prayers, and support.
-Nancy Gordon

Library of Congress Cataloging-in Publication Data

Thomason, Jean, 1969-
  The resurrection eggs / by Jean Thomason and Nancy Gordon.
    p. cm.
  Summary: Miss PattyCake recites a rhyme about many colored eggs, each of which contains something which helps to tell the story of Easter and Jesus' resurrection.
  ISBN 1-59145-054-3
    1. Jesus Christ--Resurrection--Juvenile literature. 2. Easter--Juvenile literature. [1. Jesus Christ--Resurrection. 2. Easter.] I. Gordon, Nancy, 1955- II. Title.

BT482.T48 2003
232.9'7—dc21
                                              2002191307

Printed in the United States of America
  04 05 06 LBM 9 8 7 6 5 4 3 2

A note to the reader

Eggs, eggs everywhere...not scrambled, fried, over easy or poached, but filled with a message of hope. *The Story of the Resurrection Eggs* is not a fairy tale, it's not a legend...it is the true, miraculous story of Easter! A story that is alive—a story that has changed millions of people's lives!

Welcome to the wonderful world of *preschool playtime praise* with Miss PattyCake™. Thank you for choosing to share this story of Easter with your little ones. We know that when we read to children, we are giving them a priceless gift.

Our friends at FamilyLife™ have created a fun, interactive way to tell and teach our children about the Resurrection using twelve colorful eggs. We have chosen seven of these eggs to share the story in rhyme for preschoolers. Five additional eggs/stories feature details we feel are better understood by older children. If you have the carton of Resurrection Eggs, encourage your child to open the eggs with you as you read. Your little ones will also love learning the songs while watching Miss PattyCake's *Eggstravaganza* on video or DVD. What a joy that we can share with you God's love through songs, books, videos, activities, wiggly-giggly fun, and happy hallelujahs! Miss PattyCake says:

We have two hands to clap,
one heart to love, and a voice to sing, sing, sing . . . and
Every day is a PattyCake Praise Day!

Our prayer is that the wonder of God's love will be opened to you
in a bright and colorful new way this Easter season.

- Jean and Nancy

My friends are here!

I'm so glad you're here today

To read and sing,

to laugh and play.

What does Miss PattyCake always say?

Every day is a

PattyCake praise day.

Here is Miss PattyCake's favorite song.

Clap your hands and sing along!

PattyCake Praise

PattyCake, PattyCake, clap and play.

PattyCake, PattyCake, every day.

PattyCake, PattyCake, praise the Lord.

PattyCake, PattyCake praise.

With a pat, pat, pat and a tap, tap, tap

Your little hands can clap, clap, clap.

It's a perfect day for PattyCake praise

So, pat and tap and clap, clap, clap.

Now here's a story you'll want to hear.

Are you ready to give a listening ear?

Turn the page so you can see

Just what the PattyCake plan will be.

Eggs! Eggs! Everywhere

High and low, here and there

In the grass, up and down.

Can you find them all around?

Can you count them 1-2-3?

Tell me, what colors do you see?

Orange and yellow, pink and blue,

Purple and green eggs, just for you.

These bright-colored eggs are so much fun,

They tell a story for everyone.

We'll open each one and peek inside

To find an "Eggstravaganza" surprise.

This **light blue** egg makes no sound

When you shake it all around.

Open it and what do you see?

Hmmmm . . . this egg is . . . empty!

Colonel Tick Tock says, "It's true,
This empty egg has a message for you.

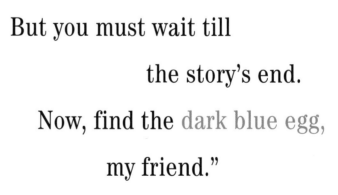

But you must wait till
the story's end.
Now, find the dark blue egg,
my friend."

In this egg I hear a sound

When I shake it all around.

Take a peek. What do you see?

Oh, look—it's a little donkey!

Clipping clopping into town

Hee haw! Hee haw!

Can you make a donkey sound?

Many people came to see

Jesus who came from Galilee.

Hosanna! They shouted on that day

As they cheered and waved Him on His way.

SHOUT HOSANNA

Can you hear the clip clop?
Can you hear the clip clop?
Can you hear the donkey
Riding into town?

Can you see Jesus?
Can you see Jesus?
Can you see Jesus
Riding up and down?

Let's skip and jump and dance and sing
Clap our hands and praise the King
Lift our hands and give a shout,
"Jesus, come and save us now."

Can you wave the branches?
Can you wave the branches?
Can you wave the branches?
Wave them while you sing.

Can you sing hosanna?
Can you sing hosanna?
Can you sing hosanna
To the King of Kings?
"Hosanna!"

The light purple egg is hiding here.

Can you find it? It's very near.

Good for you—now, open it up.

What's inside? A tiny cup.

A **table** was set with the

cup and the bread

For the Passover meal

where the **twelve** would be fed.

Jesus drank from the

cup and shared the **bread**.

"Remember me" is what He said.

Look in the orange egg and you'll find

Something we use all the time.

Hands held together in this special way

Show us that it's time to pray.

JESUS SAID YES

In the garden late that night
Jesus prayed with all His might,
"Father, help me do what's right.
I'll say yes to You.
Lord, I'll say yes to You."

Jesus said yes.
Jesus said yes.
Jesus said yes to the Father.
We can say yes.
We can say yes.
We can say yes to Him too.

I will listen when I pray,
Talk to God both night and day.
Just like Jesus I will say,
"I'll say yes to You.
Lord, I'll say yes to You."

The light yellow egg holds

something round.

It's sticky with thorns,

but shaped like a crown.

The soldiers made it for

Jesus to wear.

Then they hit Him and hurt Him;

they didn't care.

Now what's in the yellow egg?

Open it wide.

A cross, made of nails, is found inside.

The soldiers nailed Jesus' hands and His feet

To a cross where He died on Calvary.

How sad that those soldiers did not know

That Jesus, the Savior, loved them so.

They put His body into a grave,

Not down in the ground,

but more like a cave.

Then a great big stone

they rolled, rolled, rolled

In front of the cave

to cover the hole.

But that's not the end of the story—no way!

A miracle happened on the third day!

Oh, which egg will show us?

Which one should we find?

Let's ask Colonel Tick Tock.

He's here just in time.

"Open the pink egg and then you will know

What happened one morning long ago.

The rock inside is small, it's true.

But on that day the stone was HUGE!

God's power rolled that stone away

On the mighty Resurrection Day,

And Jesus Christ is no longer dead,

He's alive!

He is risen, just as He said."

MIGHTY RESURRECTION DAY

There was a shake and a rattle
And the stone was rolled away.
There was a shake and a rattle
And the stone was rolled away.
There was a shake and a rattle
And the stone was rolled away, rolled away,
On that mighty Resurrection Day
When that great big giant stone was rolled away.

The earth went to quakin'
And our knees went to shakin'.
What a mighty Resurrection Day.
And in the sky there was a rumble
When that stone began to tumble.
What a mighty Resurrection Day.
On our knees we went to prayin'
As we heard the angels sayin'
"What a mighty Resurrection Day."

Jesus is risen.
We have been given
A mighty Resurrection Day.

23

Remember the **empty egg**? Hmmm, let's think

The light blue one, and not the **pink**.

It shows that the grave

was **empty** inside,

And Jesus is not dead,

He's alive!

Let's skip and jump and dance and **sing**,

Clap our hands and praise the King.

Jesus **rose up** from that grave!

By God's miracle we are saved!

Amazing Grace can tell us why

God's Son, Jesus, had to die.

She's a wise old book, but she's **asleep**.

Let's wake her up so she can speak!

1... 2 ... 3 ... Miss Grace!

Miss Grace,
we were just wondering...
Why did Jesus have to
die on that cross?"

"Well, my dears, from the very beginning,

God has wanted each one of us to be

His very own child and live with Him forever.

But because of our sin, you know, all the wrong things we think and do,

we could never be good enough, no matter how hard we tried.

But I'm so glad that God made a way.

The Bible says in John 3:16 that

God loved the world so much

that He sent His only son, Jesus,

to die on the cross, and whoever

believes in Him will have life everlasting.

You see, nobody loves you like God,

and that's the truth."

Now you know the story of
God's great plan.

He sent His **Son** to earth for man.

Jesus died to pay for our sin

So we could

live forever with Him!

The **bright-colored eggs**

have shown you and me

Salvation's story, God's love so **free**.

His love is **not hidden;**

it's easy to find.

It's not in an egg;

it's in your heart

and mine!

It's time to sing an Easter song.

Use your voice and sing along.

March around, step up, step down,

Sing, sing, sing a happy hallelujah sound!

COLORS, NUMBERS, ABC's

(Sing to the tune of "Christ the Lord Is Risen Today")

One, two, three, four, five, six, seven

Jesus made a way to heaven.

Red and yellow, pink and blue

Jesus died for me and you.

Eight and nine and then comes ten

Jesus died and rose again.

Purple and green, now come and sing

Hallelujah to the King!

Would you like to learn more about the Easter story?
Here are five more eggs to open!

If you shake the light pink egg, you will hear a jingle and a jangle. When you open it, you will find money inside. These silver coins show us an important part of the Easter story. Some leaders wanted to kill Jesus because they were jealous of the way many of the people loved Him and followed Him. These leaders told Judas, one of Jesus' friends, that they would give him thirty pieces of silver (that's a lot of money!) if he would help them capture Jesus. Judas took the money. He was not a good friend to Jesus, was he? Then Judas showed the leaders and Roman soldiers where to find Jesus. Jesus was in a garden praying. The soldiers found Him there and took Him away.

The green egg has a small piece of leather inside. Leather like this can be used to make a whip. Today, you might see a small whip used in a horse race, but many years ago whips were sometimes used to punish people. That's what happened to Jesus. After the Roman soldiers took Jesus from the garden, the leaders asked Him many questions. Jesus told the truth, but they did not believe Him. They were angry and they hit Jesus with the leather whip. Jesus never did anything wrong and did not deserve to be hurt like that.

Look inside the light green egg and you will find a small die. We usually use this when playing games. Do you have any dice at your house? Well, dice are not new; they have been used to play games for thousands of years. Dice may seem to be a strange part of the Easter story, but here is what happened. After Jesus had been captured and whipped, the leaders said that He must die. You have already seen the cross in the yellow egg, so you know that Jesus was nailed to a cross and left there to die. While He was hanging on the cross, some of the soldiers decided to play a game. They rolled the dice, and whoever won the game got to keep Jesus' clothes as a prize.

Do you see the purple egg? It holds a tiny spear. Do you know what a spear is? It is an ancient weapon. Soldiers fought battles with spears, and the Roman soldiers of Jesus' time used them. The spear is part of the Easter story because the day Jesus died, one of soldiers at the cross held a spear. It was late in the day and Jesus had been hanging on the cross for a long time. The soldier wasn't sure that Jesus was dead, so he took his spear and stuck it in Jesus' side to make sure.

Look at the cream-colored egg. Open it and you will find a small piece of rough cloth called linen. Linen is used today to make many nice things. Long ago this cloth was part of the Easter story. After Jesus died, the soldiers took His body off the cross. An important man named Joseph loved Jesus, and made a place for Him to be buried. Joseph wrapped Jesus in a linen cloth and laid Him in a tomb. It was a sad day for Jesus' friends, but it wasn't sad for long. Jesus stayed in the tomb for three days. And then, the most wonderful thing happened! Life came back into Jesus' body! When Jesus' friends came to visit that tomb, the only thing left inside was the linen cloth.

The wonder and history of the Easter egg

Have you ever wondered why eggs became associated with the celebration of Easter? So have we! So we went on an Easter Egg History Hunt. And here is what we found: Travel back with us to the year A.D. 1000. It was a dark time in the history of the world. Although the gospel of Jesus Christ had spread to much of the known world, only a few people could read. Most people had no access to the Bible. So, much of their understanding of spiritual things was cloaked in mystery and derived from nature.

Historians tell us that in the regions now known as Northern Europe and Russia, a very strange thing happened. People noticed that in the late fall, as the days grew shorter and darker, chickens, ducks, and other poultry stopped laying eggs. This meant less food for the long, cold, hideously freezing, subzero, toe-numbing, frostbiting winter.

Now, imagine their joy when these animals suddenly began laying eggs again about the same time as the celebration of Passover and of the Resurrection! Today, we understand that this coincides with the spring equinox. But, these hungry medieval people had no explanation for why the eggs reappeared at Easter time; they simply accepted the eggs as a gift from God. Miraculous food appearing during the hungriest time of year became intertwined with the idea of new life (just like the Resurrection!). In Russia, this was called "the Miracle of the Eggs." As a result, Russians make the world's most beautiful Easter eggs, which are often covered with Christian symbols of life and resurrection.

So, this explains how chicks, baby ducks, and eggs became associated with the Christian celebration of Easter. The eggs were a symbol of God's provision and a promise of life for another year.

Wow! Isn't it marvelous to see how God used something as simple as an egg to shine His light into a dark world? Amazing . . . the natural order of creation reveals the greatness of our God!

Jean Thomason and Nancy Gordon

Be sure and share with your children
these additional products from Integrity Music,
available wherever Christian children's books, music, and videos are sold:

 Miss PattyCake and the Treasure Chest Surprise (VHS-DVD)

 Miss PattyCake Discovers Bubbling Joy (VHS-DVD)

 Miss PattyCake and the Hullabaloo Zoo (VHS-DVD)

 Miss PattyCake and the Birthday Party Surprise (VHS-DVD)

 Miss PattyCake Eggstravaganza (VHS-DVD)

 Miss PattyCake and God's Great Big World (VHS-DVD)

 Goodnight World (collection of lullabies) (CD)

 Colors, Numbers, ABC's (collection of songs) (CD)

For more fun, visit us online at **www.misspattycake.com**
Find more great music at **www.integritymusic.com** or books at **www.integritypublishers.com**

We want to thank FamilyLife™, a division of Campus Crusade for Christ, for allowing us to share the Resurrection Eggs® with you this Easter. If you would like to purchase additional cartons of Resurrection Eggs from FamilyLife™, please call 1-800-FL-TODAY or visit **www.familylife.com** on the web.

FamilyLife
Dennis Rainey, Executive Director
P.O. Box 8220
Little Rock, AR 72221-8220